For those who choose a path at night.
—A.J.

For Joseph, the last of the group. Lots of cats,
but no elephants!
—D.C.

On the following pages, turn off the lights to see what glows in the dark and answer the question next to the ☾ icon.

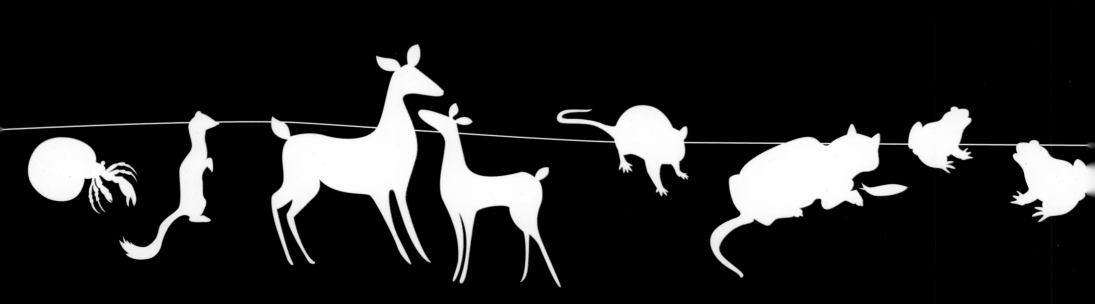

ANIMALS AT NIGHT

Anne Jankéliowitch

Delphine Chedru

sourcebooks
jabberwocky

Contents

Nighttime Mysteries

You might think that, like you, nature goes to sleep at night. In fact, a third of *vertebrates* (creatures with backbones, like you!) and two-thirds of *invertebrates* (creatures with no backbones, like bugs!) are *nocturnal*, meaning they're wide awake at night.

Diurnal animals are active during the day, while nocturnal animals are sleeping. As soon as the sun sets, nocturnal animals emerge from their hiding places and get to work!

Why do nocturnal animals like the night better than the day?

What's so great about staying up all night? It's cold, humid, and hard to see. While that might not sound like much fun to you, snails and slugs prefer it that way! That's also why they come out on rainy days.

In the desert, many animals are active at night to escape high daytime temperatures. When it's dark, nocturnal wanderers are difficult to detect and less likely to be attacked by predators. On the other hand, the darkness of the night also makes it easier for predators to prowl unnoticed and hunt their prey.

Being out and about when others are sleeping can be a good way to avoid competition. For example, nocturnal bats and diurnal swallows have similar diets, but their different schedules prevent them from competing for food.

Why do birds sing at dawn and dusk?

It's not to serenade us. Birds sing to attract a mate and procreate. The farther away their song is heard, the better. Sound carries more easily in the early morning and at twilight. During the day, heat from the sun affects the air so that birds' melodies have a much shorter range. At dusk, at night, or at dawn, air is more stable, and a bird's warbling can be heard from a greater distance. Now we know why birds burst into song at dawn!

Why do you sometimes see frogs on roads instead of in ponds?

Amphibians don't spend all their time in water. Every spring, masses of frogs *migrate*, or travel in large groups, to ponds to look for mates. They gather together at the water's edge each night, and croak, ribbit, and chirp a chorus of mating calls, much as birds do at dawn.

Amphibians like frogs lay their eggs in ponds, and the eggs become tadpoles. Once the tadpoles mature into frogs, they can leave the ponds. But when it's mating season again, frogs often have to cross a lot of roads to get back to their breeding grounds.

Why are owls such good hunters?

Owls are well-equipped for hunting. They have excellent nighttime vision and a highly developed sense of hearing. The feathers around an owl's eyes are flat like a satellite dish that channels sound toward the animal's ears. An owl can hear a small rodent moving in the grass from hundreds of yards away. Owls also have special feathers at the tips of their wings that don't rustle the grass or leaves as they fly. This means they can fly silently over fields and their prey doesn't hear them coming.

How do nocturnal animals see in the dark?

Humans depend on sight to get around, so it's hard for us to feel comfortable moving in the dark. Many animals, however,

see just as well at night as they do in broad daylight. Their vision is adapted to amplify even the tiniest amount of light.

Some small nocturnal rodents have very large eyes to pick up even more light. Other animals have a special reflective layer in their eyes to augment any light shined their way. That's why a cat's eyes sometimes appear to glow in the dark!

In addition to night vision, a nocturnal animal usually has other well-developed senses to help it get around in the dark. Some moths can smell others of their kind from

miles away. Mice and cats use their whisker to enhance their sense of touch.

A bat's vision is not as good as that of man other nocturnal animals, but bats are no really blind. They have an extra sense called echolocation. The bat calls out while flying and the sound bounces off nearby objects creating an echo. The bat picks up the echo and is able to avoid obstacles or fly straigh toward its dinner.

Still other migratory animals like toads and birds use the Earth's magnetic fields to help find their way, as though they had a compass in their heads!

IN THE FOREST

Mammals, insects, and birds all have lots to do at night. Exploring, hunting, and marking their territories... There's no time for rest!

DEER

In the morning and evening, deer leave their daytime hiding places in the forest to *graze*, or look for food, in fields and other clearings. Male deer are called *stags* and have large antlers. On autumn nights, stags look for mates by calling out to *does*, or female deer. Baby deer, or *fawns*, are born with white spots on their brown fur that disappear in adulthood.

STAG BEETLE

These beetles take their name from male deer because their *mandibles*, or jaws, look like stag antlers. They might look scary, but their young—called *larvae*—eat rotting wood, while adults feed on sap. During the summer they buzz loudly and fly low at dusk, making them easy prey for other creatures.

Whose footprints do you see on the trail?

EARWIG

During the day, earwigs hide under bark, under stones, or in flower petals. They have wings that fold up out of sight, and pincers to defend themselves and help catch their prey. Don't worry, though, they don't want anything to do with your ears! They mostly eat fruits, veggies, and flowers.

AMERICAN PINE MARTEN

The marten has a pointy brown nose and silky fur that can be pale yellow, light brown, or almost black. Nocturnal martens spend nights hunting on the forest floor for delicacies like seeds and fruit as well as insects, worms, eggs, and rodents. They're especially active during the summer months.

DORMOUSE

Dormice get their name from the French word *dormir*, "to sleep" because most species of dormouse *hibernate*, or take a long nap, for six months out of the year. Dormice have big eyes and excellent hearing, and they are very good at climbing trees to hide from owls and look for food. They are very small, growing to be two to seven inches long (including their furry tails).

AT THE FOREST'S EDGE

All night long, predators hunt for small rodents and insects, but plants are busy at night too! Some plants can glow in the dark, an ability known as *bioluminescence*.

BOBCAT (OR WILDCAT)

Bobcats have gray or brown fur, and tufted ears, and they hunt birds and small rodents. They're very stealthy, so they're hard to spot. The bobcat is very territorial; it lives and hunts in one area where it can hide in dens and raise kittens.

NIGHTJAR (OR NIGHTHAWK)

Nightjars have exceptionally soft feathers for eerily silent flight. Their pattern and coloring are good as *camouflage*, helping them blend in with bark or leaves. Some nightjars lay their eggs on the ground instead of in trees.

> What is the bobcat so interested in observing?

RED FOX

Distantly related to dogs, red foxes are very adaptable and agile. They are capable swimmers and can jump over six feet high! Foxes are no picky eaters and are happy to bound through fields in search of anything from small rodents to insects, using their acute hearing to track prey from over three hundred feet away.

GREATER MASTIFF BAT

This bat is the largest in North America and has a wingspan of over twenty-two inches. It eats insects and can live up to fifteen years in the wild. This species does not migrate or hibernate and is active all year round. You can hear its echolocation squeaks from nearly a thousand feet away.

RHINOCEROS BEETLE

Rhinoceros beetles can fly and are usually active around twilight, after their diurnal predators have gone to sleep. The males have horns that they use to fight each other in order to gain females' attention and to claim food sites. Some adult beetles can lift 850 times their weight. They typically eat rotting wood and plants, and some can grow up to seven inches long.

NEAR THE RIVERBANK

At night, rivers don't stop running, and many animals come out of hiding from piles of craggy rocks, tangles of roots, and underwater dens.

BEAVER

With waterproof fur, paddle-shaped tails, and webbed feet, beavers are natural swimmers. As *herbivores*, or creatures that eat plants, beavers love tree bark. These animal architects use their big front teeth to cut down trees to make river dams and dens called *lodges*. What may look like a pile of sticks to you may actually be a beaver's home.

EEL

Eels are long fish that look like swimming snakes. There are more than eight hundred species of eel, ranging in length from four inches to eleven feet! They burrow into mud during the day and search for small crustaceans, fish, and larvae to eat at night. Eels can live anywhere from thirty to eighty years.

> 🌙 What is the name of the insects with translucent wings flying above the river?

RIVER HERRING

The river herring, or shad, is a silvery-blue fish that lives in the ocean but is born in the river. When it's time to reproduce, it swims upstream to where it was hatched and lays its eggs at night. Females release up to 700,000 eggs in one season.

RIVER OTTER

Otters are very playful and use their sleek bodies to slide from the riverbank into the water. Like beavers, they have webbed feet and waterproof fur. They even move into empty beaver dens called *holts*, typically found under tree roots near rivers, where they teach their young, called *pups*, how to swim and fish. They are *carnivores*, meaning they eat mostly meat, particularly fish. Some otters use stones to crack open shellfish on their bellies while floating on their backs.

CRAYFISH

With their tiny claws and shells, crayfish look like little lobsters. They hide under roots or flat stones during the day. As soon as the sun sets, they go out in search of snails, worms, and tadpoles. Crayfish typically live where there is fresh running water, such as in rivers, and stream-fed lakes and swamps.

IN FIELDS AND ORCHARDS

With lots to eat and room to move about, fields and orchards are the place to be if you want to snack on fruit, seeds, and bugs all night long.

GREAT HORNED OWL

This common North American owl has feathery "horns" called *plumicorns*. Its yellow eyes, striped coloring, and three- to seven-foot wingspan make it one of the scariest predators in North America. It eats almost any rodent it can catch, as well as scorpions, frogs, and even other birds. In the morning, it settles down for the day high in any tree wherever it decides to stop hunting.

GIANT PEACOCK MOTH

Also known as the giant emperor moth, this is the largest moth in Europe, with an eight- to ten-inch wingspan. Its name comes from the four "eyespots" on its wings, which resemble a peacock's feathers. Most moths eat leaves and lay their eggs in tree and shrubs.

On what type of tree is the great horned owl perched?

HARE

Hares have longer legs and ear[s]
than rabbits, and are born i[n]
simple nests rather than in unde[r]
ground burrows. Some hares ca[n]
leap up to ten feet high and ru[n]
upwards of forty-seven miles pe[r]
hour. Normally very shy, hare[s]
hide in fields and prairies at tw[i]
light or dawn, always aler[t]

HEDGEHOG[S]

Hedgehogs are named for thei[r]
pig-like snouts and their habit [of]
hiding under tall bushes calle[d]
hedges, where they sleep durin[g]
the day and hibernate all winte[r]
Covered in about 6,000 shor[t]
pointy hairs called *quills*, they ro[ll]
into tight, spiny balls when pre[d]
ators are near. After rainfall, the[y]
rummage about in fallen leave[s]
searching for berries and insect[s]
They are native to Europe, Asi[a]
and Afric[a]

AMERICA[N]
HARVEST MOUS[E]

This very small mouse weighs si[x]
to twenty grams, while the smalle[st]
babies are only about one gram whe[n]
they're born—that's the same weigh[t]
as a paper clip! They are exceller[t]
climbers and hide in high gras[s]
where they build round, globe-lik[e]
nests. They love eating insects, flow[
ers, and seeds, and even climb up cor[n]
stalks to eat corn right off the co[b]
using their tails for balanc[e]

ON A COUNTRY ROAD

Animals must sometimes cross roads, but cars' bright headlights are blinding to nocturnal animals' light-sensitive eyes.

BADGER

With a black face that features white stripes running down its snout, it's no surprise the badger is a relative of the skunk. It has short arms for digging and strong jaws for clamping onto prey, which mainly consists of rodents. During the day, it relaxes in its *sett*, an underground burrow with many rooms and tunnels. Even with their round bodies and short legs, badgers can run up to nineteen miles per hour in short bursts to escape predators.

Turn off the lights! Do you see which parts of this scene were made by humans?

COMMON TOAD

A toad is a type of frog with dry, bumpy skin. In spring, toads migrate to ponds to find mates and lay their eggs, using the smell of water and their sense of the earth's magnetic field to figure out where to go.

RABBIT

Rabbits are prey for many animals, so they are very cautious and always alert. They use their long ears to detect the slightest noise, and their powerful legs to quickly scamper away from possible predators. Rabbits also have incredible vision, and often sleep with their eyes open so that any sudden movements will wake them up.

VOLE

This small, plump rodent has a short tail, small eyes and ears, and a round head that helps it burrow underground. Mice and voles can survive on almost any nut or fruit, but voles will often eat the roots of plants entirely from underground.

ON THE FARM

Smaller towns are often close to woods, fields, or forests, which means animals are nearby, exploring and looking for food.

BLACK RAT
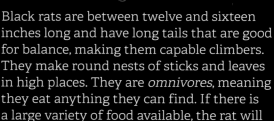

Black rats are between twelve and sixteen inches long and have long tails that are good for balance, making them capable climbers. They make round nests of sticks and leaves in high places. They are *omnivores*, meaning they eat anything they can find. If there is a large variety of food available, the rat will sample a bit of everything.

BEECH MARTEN

Beech martens, also known as stone or house martens, are found near areas of human habitation where they can make dens in buildings, tree hollows, or rock crevices. They have gray to brown fur with a white throat patch. These omnivores prefer to eat eggs, fruit, and small mammals.

Which animals are working together? Look for the animal bringing food to its mate.

BARN OWL

Barn owls are found almost everywhere in the world. They usually pick one mate for life, and one watches the nest while the other hunts. The feathers around an owl's eyes are called a facial disc—the barn owl's is shaped like a heart. When a barn owl catches prey in its talons, it swallows it and then spits out whatever it can't digest.

HOUSE LONGHORN BEETLE

This black beetle got its name because its larvae love to eat wood—including your house! It leaves visible twisting trails through wood it has eaten. At night, when it's quiet, it's even possible to hear the beetles munching.

BATS

There are more than forty species of bats in North America and, contrary to popular belief, not all of them live in caves. Some of them like the ease of hunting moths attracted to outdoor lights. Others fill up on fruit. Almost all bats have big ears to sharpen their hearing, as most bats use echolocation to find their way around. Even though all bats fly, they are not related to birds—bats are the only mammals capable of sustained flight.

IN THE NEIGHBOR-HOOD

In this urban habitat, moths swarm streetlights, owls eat rats, and cats prowl their territory like lions on the savannah—before they settle down to a dinner of canned cat food.

BROWN RAT

Also known as the street rat, this is the most common rat in the world, found on every continent except Antarctica. They live almost anywhere that humans live, and use their excellent sense of smell to find tasty tidbits that humans leave behind.

HOUSE CAT

House cats are among the most common predators of birds, rodents, and rabbits living in and around towns. Cats like settling in high places where they can lie in wait and pounce on prey. If a cat falls from a high perch, it can twist its body to land on its feet. House cats can live anywhere from seven to fifteen years on average.

What types of lights brighten the city at night?

BARRED OWL

Native to North America, this species is also known as the hoot owl for its recognizable call, which sounds like "Who cooks for you?" Its body length can range from sixteen to twenty-five inches long, with a wingspan of thirty-eight to forty-nine inches. It hunts at dawn or dusk by waiting on a high branch and swooping down on prey, which can include almost anything smaller than itself: rodents, rabbits, small birds, chickens, snakes, frogs, even turtles. You may even spot a barred owl near a campfire, looking for insects drawn by the light.

MOTHS

In North America, there are approximately twelve thousand species of moths. They often have featherlike antennae and are not usually very colorful.

COCKROACH

Cockroaches are among the hardiest insects in the world and live in a wide range of environments, even the Arctic. Some species are able to survive for up to a month without any food, while others can go without air for as long as forty minutes. Some live in or near water and breathe by poking part of their body above the surface like a snorkel, or by carrying an air bubble under their shell.

IN THE GARDEN

The household garden is a refuge for little critters that are very active when everyone in the house is asleep.

SPIDERS

Spiders are *arachnids*, which differ from insects by having eight legs rather than six. Spiders are very intelligent hunters who create their own sticky thread that they spin into elaborate webs to trap prey. All spiders are venomous predators, but of the four thousand types of spiders found in North America, only a few are dangerous to humans.

MOCKINGBIRD

The mockingbird is best known for its ability to mimic the songs of other birds, and even frogs and insects. This versatile songbird sings different tunes in fall and spring, and has been known to imitate the songs of twenty or more species within ten minutes.

Can you find the tiny creatures that make their own light? How many are there?

FIREFLY

The firefly, also known as the lightning bug, is a type of winged beetle. These *bioluminescent* bugs can produce their own light in a variety of colors from yellow and green to pale red. Their larvae are also known as glowworms. It is believed that fireflies glow to signal that they are looking for mates. Fireflies do not taste good to most predators, and are sometimes poisonous too.

MIDWIFE TOAD

This species of toad is found in parts of Europe and Africa. After the female lays the eggs, the male holds them between his back legs until they are ready to hatch. Then he sits at the edge of the water until all the tadpoles have emerged. Adults have few predators because they are covered in warts that give off a smelly poison.

GROUND BEETLE

There are over forty thousand species of ground beetle, making it one of the largest animal families in the world. Many ground beetles are shiny and brightly colored, but have no wings. This small insect lives in household gardens and forests, and prefers the cool of night for hunting snails, slugs, larvae, and worms.

MOUNTAINS

Mountains are home to many species similar to those that live elsewhere, but these animals have different abilities to help them survive.

EASTERN NEWT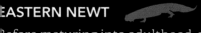

Before maturing into adulthood, a newt tadpole turns into a black-spotted, red-orange newt called a *red eft*. This coloring is meant as a warning sign to predators indicating that they are poisonous to eat! The red eft travels across the land in search of a new home, sometimes for two or three years. By the time the newt finds a muddy pond to settle down in, its adult coloring has changed to a green back and yellow belly.

STOAT (OR ERMINE)

Though small, stoats are adept predators. They are long and thin enough to follow small rodents into their homes, strong enough swimmers to catch and eat amphibians, and good enough climbers to scale trees and steal birds' eggs out of nests. Stoats make their dens in burrows or hollow trees. In the winter, the stoat turns from brown to pure white, and is known as the ermine.

How many snowy mountaintops do you see shining in the moonlight?

EAGLE OW

With a thirty-inch-long bod
and a six-foot wingspan, this i
one of the largest owls in th
world. Its plumicorns look lik
sharp, slanted eyebrows abov
its bright orange eyes. It lives i
a variety of habitats from forest
to deserts, but prefers to nes
in high, concealed locations. I
mostly hunts at dusk and dawr
and eats anything that move
including insects, frogs, fish
rodents, and even fawns

BROWN BEA

The brown bear is also known i
North America as the grizzly bea
and it is one of the largest lan
mammals in the world. Males ca
grow to be more than nine fee
tall, with huge paws eight to fou
teen inches wide! Despite the
imposing size, bears are not ver
active predators. They primaril
eat plant life, but will eat almos
anything they can find—as lon
as there's a lot of i

LYNX

A lynx is a solitary wildcat with
tufted ears and a short tail. It typ
ically builds its den in a crevice o
under a ledge. The bobcat is one
well-known species of lynx. One
theory for how the lynx got its name
is from an Old English word for *ligh*
because of its big reflective eyes
which are good for seeing in the dark

AT THE BEACH

Just under the water's surface, the ocean is teeming with life, from the biggest fish to the smallest bioluminescent plankton that light up the waves.

SLIPPER LOBSTER

This warm-water crustacean differs from spiny lobsters by its large flat antennae. Slipper lobsters can be anywhere from two to twenty inches long. They hide in crevices, caves, and reefs, and emerge at night in search of *mollusks* such as snails and slugs.

SEA ANEMONE

This creature may be named for the beautiful anemone flower, but it is actually related to jellyfish and corals (yes, corals are creatures too!). The anemone has a sticky foot to keep its body in place and toxic tentacles to ensnare and eat small fish and shrimp. An anemone can reproduce on its own by splitting its body in half.

 Do you know the name of the see-through sea creature in this picture?

 OCTOPUS

The octopus is one the most intelligent ocean creatures. It has keen eyesight and can change colors. When attacked, it ejects a cloud of dark ink, and escapes long before the water clears. It has no skeleton, so it can squeeze into the tiniest nooks and crannies to escape predators or pursue prey.

CONGER

A marine eel that can grow up to ten feet long and weigh up to 240 pounds, the conger's size and many teeth make it a fearsome nocturnal predator—even to humans! It hides under rocks or sunken ships, and comes out at night to strike at crustaceans, fish, and octopi that pass by.

 HERMIT CRAB

The hermit crab lives in a shell that it drags wherever it goes. As the crab grows, it needs larger and larger shells to live in. When it finds one, it will leave its own shell to inspect the larger one. If it doesn't fit, it will wait for another crab to appear, and take that crab's shell instead! Sometimes, a small anemone will stick to a hermit crab shell in order to get a ride through the sea, which also encourages predators to stay away. This relationship is *symbiotic*, meaning the hermit crab and the anemone help each other out.

IN THE DESERT

Animals that live in the desert have numerous adaptations to the heat, just as nocturnal animals are adapted to the dark.

SCORPION

The scorpion has big claws for seizing prey, and a venomous stinger at the tip of its tail to protect itself from predators. Its sting can be painful but only a few species are dangerous to humans. This hardy arachnid can be found on every continent except Antarctica. Scorpions are also *fluorescent*; they glow blue-green when exposed to ultraviolet light!

RATTLESNAKES

The rattlesnake is a venomous viper that rattles the hollow scales at the tip of its tail to scare off predators. Rattlesnakes are not aggressive, however, and will only attack if provoked. A rattlesnake's diet typically includes rodents, lizards, and birds. It has a kind of heat "vision," which enables it to sense body heat and accurately strike its target in total darkness.

Do you know the name of the animal whose legs and tail are glowing in the dark?

FENNEC FOX

This is a very small nocturnal fox native to the Sahara Desert. Its body is typically only nine to sixteen inches long, but its ears can be four to six inches long, and it can hear insects and small animals moving even underground. Multiple families of fennec foxes live together in vast networks of dens dug into sand. They pick one mate for life, and males become very protective of females after mating.

JERBOA

With its extra-long ears, legs, and tail, the jerboa resembles a mouse-sized kangaroo! When it's hot outside, the jerboa stays buried in the sand. At nightfall, it comes out to nibble on grasses and the occasional insect. Though hunted by snakes, foxes, and owls, its huge ears help it hear when predators are coming, and it hops away quick as can be.

ADDAX

Native to the Sahara, the addax is a type of spiral-horned antelope that is well adapted to desert life and can go long periods without water. Led by the oldest female, addax herds track rainfall from miles away. They hide in nests dug into sand during the day and graze at night. The addax is a critically endangered species due to excessive poaching by humans.

BY THE POND

In spring, it's hopping at the pond! Animals mate, lay eggs, chase prey, and gather leaves to make nests.

MUSKRAT

The muskrat is a large amphibious rodent. Its body is up to thirteen inches long with a flat, scaled tail that can be as long as the body. An excellent swimmer, it's covered in two layers of fur that help keep it dry. It constructs twig lodges with underwater entrances among the reeds it likes to eat, and also has the intelligence to open shellfish.

HERON

Some herons are diurnal and some are nocturnal, but both kinds are found at the water's edge to prey upon small fish, crustaceans, and insects. Herons migrate annually in search of new feeding grounds. Male herons attract females by beginning to build nests, which the mates then finish together.

 Which animal is the same color as the moon's reflection?

MAYFLY

Mayflies hatch together in large numbers at dawn or dusk throughout the spring and summer. The presence of their larvae, known as *nymphs* or *naiads*, by freshwater ponds indicates a clean, unpolluted environment. Most mayflies live for less than a day. Their only goal is to reproduce, but they are also an important and abundant food source to birds and fish.

POLECAT

Despite the name, polecats are actually more closely related to dogs than cats! The polecat resembles a large ferret with a white face and white-tipped ears. It mainly eats small rodents but also hunts amphibians and birds. When threatened, the polecat releases a very smelly spray, like a skunk. The common polecat is primarily found on the British Isles, but in the United States, the name "polecat" refers to a skunk.

AMERICAN BULLFROG

The bullfrog can weigh up to two pounds and grow over eight inches long. It has powerful hind legs and can jump ten times its body length. It eats enormous amounts of fish, birds, reptiles, and bats. The male's call sounds like a cow mooing, which is how the bullfrog gets its name.

Answers

Originally published as *Petits Animaux de la Nuit*, © De La Martinière
Jeunesse, part of La Martinière Groupe, Paris, 2016. Translated from French by
Eve Bodeux.

Published by Sourcebooks Jabberwocky, an imprint of Sourcebooks, Inc.
P.O. Box 4410, Naperville, Illinois 60567–4410
(630) 961–3900
Fax: (630) 961–2168
sourcebooks.com

Library of Congress Cataloging-in-Publication data is on file with
the publisher.

Source of Production: Leo Paper, Heshan City, Guangdong Province, China
Date of Production: June 2017
Run Number: 5009690

Printed and bound in China.
LEO 10 9 8 7 6 5 4 3 2 1